THE MEANING OF WAITING

Victoria Brittain

THE MEANING OF WAITING

TALES FROM THE WAR ON TERROR

Prisoners' Wives Verbatim

OBERON BOOKS
LONDON

First published in 2010 by Oberon Books Ltd
521 Caledonian Road, London N7 9RH
Tel: 020 7607 3637 / Fax: 020 7607 3629
e-mail: info@oberonbooks.com
www.oberonbooks.com

A catalogue record for this book is available from the British
Library.

ISBN: 978-1-84943-051-7

Cover photography by Dan Colcer

Printed in Great Britain by CPI Antony Rowe, Chippenham.

With gratitude to Sabah, Josephine, Dina, Zinnira, Hamda, Ragaa, Wendy, Amani and Saiyeda

Guantanamo Bay

A "war on terror" was declared by President George Bush in the aftermath of the 9/11 attack on the United States. The US bombing of Afghanistan, the fall of the Taliban government, a chaotic exodus of refugees into Pakistan, and a world-wide hunt by the US for Osama Bin Laden and his associates, led thousands of muslims to prisons, interrogation centres, and torture chambers in many countries.

On January 11 2002, Muslim prisoners from Afghanistan began being deported by the US to Guantanamo Bay, a prison camp in Cuba where the US retained sovereignty and a military base. Guantanamo was termed a place where the US constitution did not apply.

For four years even the names of most of the prisoners were kept secret.

The 774 prisoners were designated "enemy combatants," and the Geneva Conventions were declared not to apply to them. Many dozens of men were subjected to "extraordinary rendition" to countries such as Jordan, Egypt, Morocco and Syria where they were interrogated under torture. Another 94 were held in secret prisons run by the CIA in countries such as Afghanistan, Poland and Romania for several years. Twenty eight of these were designated as "high value detainees" and 14 of them were transferred to Guantanamo Bay in September 2006.

Many of the prisoners were handed over to the US in exchange for "bounties" of $5,000 offered for foreigners, particularly Arabs. A study by Seton Hall Law School in the US found that 86% of detainees were not picked up on the battlefields, but captured by Pakistani authorities or the Afghan Northern Alliance. Others were picked up by the Americans in countries as far afield as Bosnia, Gambia, Zambia, often in cooperation with British Intelligence, and flown to prisons in Kandahar and Bagram before ending in Guantanamo Bay.

In June 2004, after prolonged legal battles by US lawyers, the US Supreme Court ruled that men held in Guantanamo had the right to have their cases heard in federal courts. By April 2010 rulings on the prisoners' *habeas corpus* petitions had been made by US judges in 46 cases. In 34 of these, the judges ruled that the government had failed to demonstrate that the men had any connection to al-Qaeda or the Taliban. Nevertheless, the vast majority of those still held had no idea when, if ever, they would get out. President Obama's promise to close the camp within a year of taking office was broken, and no new deadline set.

In July 2010, 181 prisoners were still in Guantanamo Bay.

In July 2010, the new coalition goverment in Britain announced that an inquiry was to be set up under Sir Peter Gibson – a former appeal court judge – into the involvement of the British government and security services in the torture and abuse of terror suspects held in other countries.

'Control orders'

Control orders are – as their name suggests – orders which control people by subjecting them to restrictions on their daily lives. They are applied to persons suspected of involvement in terrorism or support for terrorism, who the security services say cannot be prosecuted.

After 9/11, foreign suspected terrorists who could not legally be deported because of the risk they would be tortured in their home countries were detained indefinitely in high security prisons.

In December 2004, the judicial committee of the House of Lords (now the Supreme Court) ruled indefinite detention unlawful, since it applied only to foreigners, and not to British terrorist suspects.

In March 2005 Control Orders were introduced, and are applied both to British terrorist suspects and to foreign suspects who cannot be deported.

A typical control order contains a 16-hour curfew (meaning that the controlled person must stay in his accommodation for 16 hours a day, eg from 6pm to 10am – and permission is needed even to go into the garden in curfew hours); an electronic tag, worn round the ankle, to allow monitors to track movements; an obligation to report to monitors before leaving the accommodation and on return; a geographical boundary beyond which movement is prohibited; advance vetting of all visitors; restrictions on meetings outside the home; no mobile phone, computer or telecomms equipment except for one land-line phone; restriction to one bank account. The orders are imposed for a year at a time, and some controlled persons have been controlled for five years.[1]

---

1 For more on the impact of control orders and national security deportation see Victoria Brittain, 'Besieged in Britain', *Race and Class* (2009) 50:3. Institute of Race Relations

A high court judge has to give permission before a control order is made, but the proposed controlled person is given no notice and no chance to challenge the order in advance. It generally takes over a year for the controlled person's challenge to be heard in the courts, during which time all the restrictions are in force.

The controlled persons are generally given very little information about the reasons for the order. Frequently the allegation has been in very general terms, eg 'It is assessed that you have been engaged in attack planning', with no further details.

Until 2005 the government accepted that foreign terrorist suspects could not be returned to states such as Algeria, Jordan and Libya because of the serious risk of torture. But in that year, the government began to seek diplomatic assurances from these countries that they would accept national security deportees from the UK and not torture them, and after concluding agreements, began the process of returning deportees to these countries. The courts have ruled that Libya is not safe, and national security deportations to the other countries are suspended while applications to the European Court of Human Rights are pending. Meanwhile, the proposed deportees are detained in high security prison, often for years. If released, they are subjected to even more stringent conditions than Control Orders, with curfews of up to 22 hours a day, and in one case 24 hours a day.

The play was first produced as *Waiting*, at the Purcell Room on March 12 and 13 2010, by the Southbank Centre in association with Metta Theatre Company. The production text of *Waiting* was a modified version of the original *The Meaning of Waiting*.

Director, Dramaturge and Librettist, Poppy Burton-Morgan *
Composer, Jessica Dannheisser *
Design, Projection and Lighting, William Reynolds
Assistant Director, Rachel Warr

SABAH, Juliet Stevenson
WENDY, Gemma Jones
ALEXIA, Simone James
NOUR *(Soprano)*, Anna Dennis
YASMINE *(Mezzo)*, Carole Wilson
CELLO, Oliver Coates
WOMEN A, Harriet Ladbury
WOMAN C, Diana Hardcastle
WOMAN Z, Manjinder Virk

After each performance there was a panel discussion, with Baroness Helena Kennedy QC, Salma Yacoob, Gareth Peirce, Vanessa Redgrave, Manjinder Virk, Riz Ahmed, Moazzem Begg, chaired by Victoria Brittain.

Flowers were presented to four of the women in the audience whose words were spoken.

The libretto for the two sung characters, Nour and Yasmine, was taken from the text.

The Meaning of Waiting was published in Arabic in Beirut by Dar Al Furabi in 2009, with a translation by Maha Bahbou funded by the Qattan Foundation in Ramallah.

www.mettatheatre.co.uk

www.jessicadannheisser.com

Characters

Alexia	French/Senegalese
Sabah	British/Palestinian
Yasmine	British/Jordanian
Nour	British/Palestinian
Wendy	British
Amani	British/Libyan
Woman A	
Woman B	
Woman Z	

Backdrop of images of completely veiled women in black in what is recognizably London. Outside Regents Park Mosque on a Friday just before prayer time. Edgware Road restaurants with men sitting outside, smoking hookahs, reading papers, talking. Women in black veils are walking by, with lots of children, stopping at fruit and vegetable shops with produce piled high on pavement.

Intercut images of East African embassy bombings, 9/11 New York, London 7/7, and, very briefly, massed London policemen, and police cars and vans. Silent.

Black.

Lights go up and onto a woman in dark long coat with white head veil, SABAH, sitting as though at a kitchen table. At the front of the stage, on the side, is another, ALEXIA, fully veiled in a dark brown robe and face veil. She is sitting in the doorway of her flat. Each one speaks to the audience as though the other was not there.

ALEXIA: It was about six in the morning and my husband was in the living room because it was nearly time for prayer, they came, and one lady in a suit switched on the light and I wake up. I turned for my *hijab*.......
I want to know what happened, and she was telling me, just wait a minute. I didn't understand anything, I heard voices, and there was people walking and they was talking with my husband.

My husband came to the door and they didn't let him into my room. He asked me to pack up his bag, and I tell him, 'What happened?' And he tell me, 'They coming in to arrest me.' And I say, 'Why?' I start to really panic. He says, 'They are arresting me on suspicion of terrorism.' At this time I didn't understand good English, I didn't understand anything, nothing. So I am starting to cry, and he said, 'Just make my bag.' And then, they left,....... they took him......., they handcuff him, and they let him just tell me, 'Bye.'

SABAH: I hate to hear knocking on the door. My heart leaps and knocks, and I remember that time when the police came in the night after my husband was away. There were dozens of them, everywhere, upstairs, downstairs.

My Mum, that night........she was completely white, no colour, when she saw these police inside our house, in the middle of the night.

I never like to see police after this experience, I remember it whenever I see them.

They took us away, to a hotel – all my little children in their night clothes, so scared and not understanding, none of us understanding, anything.

One thing I'll never forget is how the
people there looked at us, when we
came into that hotel with police. They
looked……as though we were criminals. It
was horrible. I couldn't bear my Mum to be
living this.

* * * * * *

(Speech very different in these flashback stories – fluent, keen to communicate, no hesitations.)

ALEXIA: *I was born in France, but we used to go to my country sometimes, to Senegal. That's where I became muslim – just me and my sister, not the rest of the family.*

My father had many wives, five wives – it's the custom in my country, not just for muslims. The French one lived in her house in the countryside in France. The three Senegalese lived in the same house, like sisters, I called them all Mum, all the same care for us children and we same like sisters, sisters. We were always happy together.

I used to play basketball – that's what I liked, I really liked. I'm tall, so I was really good.

And it was nice here in England, you can wear a scarf and noone looks, it's not like France, its too hard being muslim there. I take my scarf off when I go on the Eurostar to visit my Mum.

I met my husband at my friend's house – it was love – he has a beautiful face, and always smiling and laughing. And it was easy for my family to accept, you know, my father had one Algerian wife too.

SABAH: *I was a school teacher in Jordan, I loved my job, and the children loved me. I was always a very happy girl, but I was also careful about my life and my family. Even then I always used to think about Allah and what he would want from me. He was always there for me in my life, in my thoughts. I started to wear the scarf when I was fourteen, although my father tried to stop me, he said it was too early and I would probably change my mind. But I insisted, I knew what I wanted. I went on the Haj with my Mother – that was a very special time for me..*

I knew that I wanted to marry a man who was very special, very pure, very good. My husband's sister knew me from the school, and my family, and when he came from working in Pakistan, wanting

17

*to get married, she asked for me,
and he came to visit my family. I
saw him, and I liked him. He's a
Palestinian, like me.*

*When I got married, he was staying
one month in Jordan before he
went back to Pakistan. We stayed
at his mother's house, and he
made this new bedroom for me, all
white, new bed, and with pink on
the curtains. I told him it wasn't
important, I could sleep on the
floor, but he wanted to do that for
me. My mother was so happy when
she came and saw that room. He
would be loving and kind with me.*

*After I was married I started
to cover my face too, as well as
wearing hijab. I always like the
feeling, – it's a very nice feeling.*

*My father didn't want me to go so
far away, to Pakistan, but I told
him, I have to be with my husband
now, I have to go with him,
however far away it is.*

*I taught school there too. Then we
had to leave – all the Arabs were
leaving suddenly – and we came*

*here to England, as refugees. Why
England? We thought it was safe.*

*I had a very long wait for my first
child, then God gave me four more,
three boys, two little girls. My life.*

*I always knew how much my
husband loves me, and the
children. This is my life. I love my
husband so much, only God knows
how much I thank him for that.*

YASMINE and NOUR enter, they are in black robes
and veiled, but take them off as they start to speak.
They are not aware of the presence of each other or
anyone else.

YASMINE: *When I was a child in
Jordan I was never away from
my family, my six sisters and four
brothers. I was the oldest girl, and I
was special, beloved......*

*I had long curly thick hair, so long
it was below my waist, so I could sit
on it – the sort of hair that mothers
love to brush and brush.*

*We were brought up in such a
tradition of manners, and of
respect for them, the mother, the
grandmother, to kiss their hand,
always to sit lower than them. We*

*were always together – every minute
– always smiling, always laughing.
Then I wore mini skirts, pretty
clothes – I was so slim then, slim
like a finger, slimmer even than any
of my daughters are now.*

*And I was the family bookworm,
always with books. I never learned
to cook from my mother, she left
me studying. The kitchen was the
centre of everything in our home –
the scents from it went everywhere,
and there was always my mother,
cooking with spices, honey, nuts....,
and love, how she loved me.*

*She couldn't be apart from me, my
mother....., nor my grandmother.*

*If she sent me on an errand, my
grandmother would say," I spit on
this stone, and I want to see you
back before it dries".*

*Our house was always open, 24
hours a day, anyone could come
for our hospitality – this is normal
happy life for us.*

*When the Palestinians came after
the nakba in 1948, we shared*

*everything with them, land, house,
food, everything. Tradition ruled
everything, helping neighbours,
anyone in need. That was what
we did naturally. This was the life
– busy, happy, safe, all together.*

*My husband's mother and my
father were cousins, but we hardly
saw his family, they lived in a
different town, not Kerik, where
I come from, near the Dead Sea.
Later I found out that my husband
saw me when he was about 14 and
decided then that I was the one for
him. I didn't know, and I never
thought about him like that. When
he proposed we were both 19 and he
told me he'd had me in his mind for
years.. It was so lovely......, feelings
you can't express. For our wedding
I had seven wedding dresses, each
one just to wear for ten minutes
or so, walking round the women's
room with everyone singing and
dancing for me. The main one was
white, of course, then there was a
red one, a golden/orange one, baby
blue, a very very light sort of pink,
no, not pink, apricot, blue blue,
and, what was it...? Afterwards I*

21

used to wear them for parties – I loved them all..

We went to Pakistan for his studies. I was so very, very, upset to go. And my mother was, maybe even more than me. I was scared....., it was the first time I left home......, the first sacrifice I had to make.

There in Pakistan I was like sitting on hot coals all the time – I couldn't wait for him to finish so we could get home to Jordan – to be with my mother and my family all around me – my old happy life.

But things were tense in Jordan when we got back, it was around the Gulf War time. My husband liked wearing that loose Pakistani clothes, very comfortable, but that didn't help – the police didn't like that – they were looking for people they could say were extremists.

He was arrested.

Of course I knew...., I knew, they tortured him. For months he was gone.

When I saw him, he was partly paralysed.

I thought my happy life was lost.

The Red Cross gave evidence for him, of what had happened to him in prison, when he came to Britain, and he was given refugee status. That was in 1991.

We felt safe here in London. It was a relief, like a drink of cool water.

NOUR: *When I was first married it was very, very hard......... I'd never, ever, been alone in my life in Jordan – always with my three sisters and four brothers. Then, I was in Pakistan and I had to stay alone by myself in our house when my husband went out. It was specially difficult in the night when he went out to the mosque.*

But you know, Islam teaches submission, and I accepted it.

And my husband was a very kind man. We were happy in Pakistan, I taught school, and Mohamed did what he loves to do, help people, like orphans – everyone he can

*identify with from his life in Gaza
– that's where he comes from, and
I'm Palestinian too, from Hebron..*

*We left in a hurry, everyone did,
suddenly the Pakistan government
was having a problem with Arab
people – it was after the Soviets
were defeated in Afghanistan.. I
don't even know why we came here
to England, my husband never
discussed it with me. I suppose
it was because his friends were
coming.*

* * * * * *

Dark.

At the back of the stage on CCTV a very thin man in a wheelchair, with a longish beard, big black eyes. His body language is very defeated, like a prisoner. He doesn't move much, just looking. He could be ALEXIA's husband, or YASMINE's, or NOUR's.

Lights up, CCTV image stays.

ALEXIA: I first saw him nearly six months after he was arrested. Six months…..being at home without him, not knowing anything – here I am in England just with my daughter… how much I was hugging her in those days. Only when the solicitor phoned, there was someone who knew what to do for me.

When I went to visit my husband, there in Belmarsh, he was in a special unit, AA. He was locked up in his cell 23 hours, he was just allowed an hour's going to the PT.

He was behind the glass. I couldn't touch him even. I spoke over a phone, and there was someone with me to translate, and someone with him as well to write down and translate everything, and a police officer as well. I speak French with him – I'm French. But what can you say to him when you see your husband like that? I cant even imagine this life he is having away from me.

Later on I saw him behind the glass,
with the phone to speak in, but without
translator.

After that I saw him in a big room with
everybody, and he can hold my daughter
on his knee, and we can have coffee, but he
can't stand up with us.

The first time I used to see him just 45
minute, then it was 30 minute, and then in
the big room it was two hours, two or three
hours I had him. That was my life.

Do you know? They never ever questioned
him, never asked him about anything. So
why was he there? What did they want to
keep him for? Noone could tell me.

He was using his crutches at this time – he
had polio when he was young.

He was…. he was starting to be too much
depressed, too depressed. Prison was killing
him slowly.

But me? Well, maybe women are different,
we have to be strong for children.

SABAH: I knew my husband was taken by
Americans, but I didn't know anything
about Guantanamo – just the terrible
pictures on TV, those orange suits, those
lines of men with blindfold in airplanes,
but I couldn't believe ever that's my
husband. Then we never heard of prisons in
Afghanistan where they took my husband.

My Mum left for Jordan just before my last baby was born, her visa had run out and we couldn't get an extension, she was so scared that she would never see me again if she overstayed, so she just went back, although she really, really, wanted to stay with me for when the baby came.

My Mum's a diabetic, worry is really bad for her. I told her, I'll be fine, don't worry, Allah will send me help.

But, once she was in the taxi for the airport – I cant forget that minute – I looked through the window and I sat down on the sofa and just cried and cried, then I went and cried on my bed.

I prayed and prayed that the baby would come in the day, not in the night. And it was in the afternoon that the waters broke, and I called the ambulance and my friend who was going to take the children. I had four children with chicken pox. They both arrived in 10 minutes, and I begged my friend's husband to look after my children – I didn't like showing what I was feeling. I gave him my keys, my purse, my bank account number, my card and my pin number, and told him, if anything happens to me, look after my children.

But then, when I got in the ambulance, there was a nurse stroking my forehead, and reading the Koran to me – can you imagine I got a muslim nurse? I'd said to my Mum, my God would help me. Always in my life it's like that, Allah knows everything best for me.

YASMINE: In January 2006, they came to our house, in the night, and they took my husband to Belmarsh – even the people who came for him were surprised to find they were taking a sick man, in a wheelchair. He is diabetic, still sick from the torture in Jordan, he has to have a very careful diet, massage, all this we can manage in the family because he's a specialist physiotherapist himself, and all my daughters are there to help me.

They refused him bail or even house arrest, and that secret court you have here, it said my husband was a member of an Islamist extremist group linked to extremist activity in the UK and overseas. But even his lawyer could not be told what they said against him in that special secret court. And the police never ever asked him anything. Never any one question. So what is he accused of? That's what I ask myself, round and round in my head.

Where is his dignity? Or mine? In that place for criminals.

Then he had a brain haemorrage and in the
hospital the doctor told us to say goodbye,
he couldn't live, but I prayed and we
massaged him. He lived, very fragile. But
then they took him back to prison without
telling us.

ALEXIA: So in that secret court, the SIAC
court, I saw my husband, very sick looking,
and the judge granted him bail. He was the
first of all of them to be granted bail. The
judge, I remember him, Judge Collins, he
said to me he want us to have a normal
family life with our daughter. Normal.

It was in April. But Brahim didn't come
home after the court that day…… because
the Home Office appealed against the
judgement.

And it took from April until end of June
until he came out of prison. Then his
health deteriorated too much, he was too
weak…… and when he came out, that's
when he goes to a wheelchair. Because his
weight dropped too much. He lost nearly
20 kilos.

Then, he stayed nine months in house
arrest, a very strict house arrest. He couldn't
go out at all. For nine months, not at all.
Doctor, hospital, nothing. No visitor at
all. Even my daughter and me, no visitors.
Even the solicitor, it took maybe three
months to be cleared to come and visit him.

And he was not allowed to have any phone, even the home phone, he was not allowed. He was not allowed to go to the garden as well. He has something like a watch on his foot, on his right leg actually. It is a tag, and everywhere he goes, it tells them. And he have to call five times a day to the tag company to say that he is still in the house. It was every four hours. The last one was the middle of the night. It is nonsense. He had the tag on at home and he had still to call five times.

This drive him mad.

At first he was very, very happy to go out of prison and be home with me and my daughter, but after three months, four months, like this, to stay at home like this, it drive you mad.

He was sleeping a lot or just watching TV. He had many pills.

And it came at a really bad time, I was pregnant and I had to do everything outside. When the washing machine broke down. I asked to have the man come to repair it. It took them, I don't know how many weeks, to arrange a man to be cleared to come and to fix it. And when the man came my husband couldn't stay in the kitchen, he had to go to the other room.

As I say, I was pregnant, but the baby died. I had to go to the hospital.

It was the harshest time, the nine months, it was very, very tough. Tough.

Then, the House of Lords, they made all the Belmarsh prisoners go free – his group – and they were on Control Order. They had the tag and all the other restrictions, but they could go out of the house from seven in the morning until seven in the evening, so then my husband had the same condition and he could go out. After the house arrest, this seemed like a new happy time for us, with my daughter.

I believed we could be happy again.

NOUR: I never knew why my husband went to Belmarsh prison – noone knew, not him, not the solicitors. What was his life in there? He couldn't cope without a future. So, you know, then my husband was in a prison hospital, Broadmoor, they took him there from Belmarsh – he got so upset there and tried to…… hurt himself.

Then when he came home from Belmarsh and Broadmoor my husband had this idea that he wanted to go to the media, and be on Al Jazeera, all the time, "its my story, its my case, I have to tell it."_

I was very, very upset when I saw my husband in the media. I don't like my children to be in that situation, with other kids saying to them, ""I saw your Dad…"

That was when he started to be very controlling of me, and of the children...... even of the clothes we wear, when we go out, everything.

We just weren't used to it, three and half years without him – of course it was terrible he was in prison – but we'd learned another way to live here, we had a beautiful time, being free, coming and going and never asking anyone.

You know, in prison he was the one who helped anyone who was sick, he took care of the men having the hardest time – the men loved him for his kindness, but outside – they took that from him, his friends could not visit him, he could not visit them – his world in London was shrunk too small.

Enter WENDY, unveiled, standing by herself, talking to the audience.

WENDY: I started to write to many of the muslim prisoners I saw on a list of those detained under the terrorism laws. I got quite a number of replies. One I didn't get a reply from was Detainee P, who, little did I imagine it, was to become my husband. I didn't know then that he was unable to reply.

He is very disabled, he lost both his forearms, and one leg is damaged too, with the bone and muscle gone. It happened in Algeria, his country. He doesn't talk about it. He doesn't talk about the past at all. He came here as an asylum seeker in 1999.

He was first arrested in 2001 and held in Belmarsh for three months with all that group, but the police never questioned him, and he was released without charge after three months. He'd got very, very depressed. Had to be in Broadmoor Secure Mental Hospital even.

ALEXIA: Brahim, he's called Mr G by the Home Office. It's strange, why did they even take away his name?

They come and arrest him for the second time, in August, 11th August 2005.

(CCTV showing news flash London 7/7, replacing wheelchair man)

It was because the July 7/7 happened. We saw it on the TV, and I turned round to my husband and asked him, can they bring you back to prison with this happening? In fact even my solicitor, she was sitting there just then, and she said, no, no, no.

One month after that, they bring him back to prison, but this time in Long Lartin, Worcestershire, it's very far. So I am alone with my daughter again, just waiting for him.

YASMINE: My husband is called Detainee OO now. But he is not just an anonymous man, in Jordan he had his own clinic for physiotherapy, he had machines from Germany, he travelled a lot and he had visas in his passport for Saudi Arabia, Pakistan.....and the UK. He is a descendant of the Prophet Muhammad.

Before this, everyone respected him, people were always coming here for his advice. I was always cooking for visitors. That was my normal life – almost just like at home in Jordan.

What is normal now? He is there, he is alone, paranoid, noone can tell him why he is there.

I have to wait.

Waiting, yes, that's what I do.

One and half years, sitting here waiting for the phone to ring, waiting for my husband.

Now he doesn't phone any more. He doesn't let us visit any more. He doesn't let the solicitor either.

I don't know what is happening to him, not seeing him, not hearing from him. I just have my thoughts about him to live with. About him now. Memories, I don't think of.

Now I don't know my husband, my own husband, inside his head. He is not the same man. I live with his silence, and with knowing he is not himself. He was seeing djinns, and bad people looking for him, that's what he told me. How could my husband speak about such things? This is not him. My husband, I know him inside out – before.

ALEXIA: Brahim stayed there in Long Lartin until the end of October, but it was too much for him and he became depressed, and he try…. he made an attempt to end of his life. How to tell?

He tried to hang himself. To hang himself from his wheelchair.

And when they find him, all his neck was blue and everything.

I went to the court when they ask again for bail.

So, the judge grants him bail again, and he came back home. It was house arrest again. But this time we have the phone, he can talk to his Mum in Algeria, he could go in the garden, just in the garden. When he came back I was pregnant, again, and in the beginning I was very sick, and I went to hospital for one month and a half.

So they relaxed his conditions and let him go and bring my daughter to school and go to do shopping and pick her up. And they gave him permission to come to the hospital with me when I have my baby – they gave it one day, and then very next day the baby came, and my husband was with me – that made me so happy.

After, they gave him just two hours to go out, from a quarter past twelve until quarter past two. He could go to the Mosque, pray in the Mosque. All this time before, he was not allowed to go praying in the Mosque. Even when it was the Eid celebration.

There is a limit to where he can go now. And always I am thinking they can come and take him. Any time he goes outside, he has to call them on the special phone, and when he comes back home he has to call them again. He presses the button for them and tells them, "Okay, its number xx and I'm going out," or, when he comes back, the same.

And of course, if he were ten minutes late or something, then, ah, he's in breach of his conditions and he can go back to prison. Yes, it's very tough. We know people who that happened to – they're back in Belmarsh

NOUR: After he came home after Belmarsh and Broadmoor he was a completely changed person.

Then he had a tag on his leg, and he had to phone the tag company so many times in the day, and even in the night, and sometimes the company would just come, or the police, saying the machine wasn't working.

There was so much tension at home, for me, for him, for everyone.......and I was so worried would he suddenly go back to prison if the phone wasn't working and the police thought he was out?

At the beginning people outside, like at the mosque, thought the tag was a recorder. They didn't want to talk to him ..... they'd be recorded by the Home Office, they thought.

And no visitors were allowed in the house, and he couldn't make any arrangement to see anyone. He could only meet his friends by chance. Can you imagine trying to understand these rules?

He had a curfew, he had to be home at 7 too.

He was very, very nervous, he used to get angry suddenly, he would shout, sometimes he broke things. He was so impatient. It was so hard for my children to see their father like that. For me.....well....what can I say?

When he was on the Control Order I stayed at home all the time, really all the time....,. (long pause)

My husband tried to hurt himself again..... several times. Well, to kill himself, that's what he said he wanted.

ALEXIA: The tagging company, they come every two weeks or so to check it, that the tag is working properly. Any time they come, we have to open up, and they can come any time of the day or night, whenever they want. Most of the time they come at night time, like, the last time they came, it was nearly 10.15, and when they left my house it was half past midnight.

There are two big black boxes in my house for the tagging company, and one of them is in my bedroom, and one of them is in the living room. We have just a one bedroom flat here, and so when they come they check the box in the bedroom, but my daughter is sleeping there, and so every time they come, they are always disturbing her.

My husband can go out through the flat into the garden, from one o'clock until four o'clock, but it's just to one part of the garden, near our flat. And if he does go into the garden, he is not allowed to talk to anyone else there.

But if people come to the front door of my house, there, he's allowed to speak with them. He can speak like I am speaking to you now, sitting in the doorway – without you can enter.

WENDY: When my husband, well, he wasn't then my husband, came out on a Control Order – with the electronic tag and all the usual conditions – he was taken to a flat in north London which was not in any way modified for someone with no forearms. The only phone was connected to the monitoring company, and he couldn't use it. So, there was Mr P, alone with no means of communication.

He had carers who came in for half an hour night and morning. Otherwise he was entirely on his own.

He had problems trying to register with a library or a dentist as his identity papers were still with the police. Friends were reluctant to visit – clearing with the Home Office is not what everyone wants to do – too intrusive.

I did get cleared to visit finally, but I only met him once before he disappeared after 7/7. That visit, when I saw him, well, I liked him. That day, when I first met him at the flat, I was a bit embarrassed. I'd never met anyone on a Control Order before, and I was by myself, and I didn't know how long I could stay, or I should stay. It was a long journey coming down from Wellingborough too.

What happened was that we just found we could really talk easily – and I'm not someone who does talk easily to people usually. I didn't feel romantic or anything. I did feel comfortable, and so did he. I ended up staying, then he went out and I went with him. We had lunch together. I was going to see him again in a month. I was *really* looking forward to it.

Finally – after 7/7 – we found he was in Long Lartin prison and facing deportation to Algeria. He was depressed, he was anxious, despairing really, and suffering flashbacks. He could easily have harmed himself, I knew. I offered to visit him in Long Lartin – it was Long Lartin wasn't it? But he didn't want me to see him there.

SABAH: For so many years I hardly even had a letter from my husband. I would write through the Red Cross, tell him about the children, send him pictures they draw, photos of them. I was always ringing the Red Cross, but they always say, "sorry, nothing for you."

I knew nothing, just watching Al Jazeera and the orange suits, not like men, not like my husband could be.

I try not to watch television, its too upsetting, always those terrible pictures of Guantanamo, and I see Abu Ghraib pictures, and I have to pray it is not like that for my husband, but I cant know. I ask people," do they hurt him there in Guanatanamo?" But, noone knows.

Once, I went to the zoo with my daughter's class from school. She was so happy, so excited, running to see animals she never saw, like giraffe. I was smiling for her, but inside I was only thinking of those cages, and my husband in his cage......

In my dreams I see my husband always. My husband in my dreams is how he always was, I see him coming back, I see him walking, smiling to me.

WENDY: Then in December 2005 he was released under very strict conditions –a tag obviously, and only two hours out a day, though later it was made three hours. Those months many things were wrong in the flat – the bathroom floor collapsed, the drains overflowed, and every time he had to wait about three weeks before the Home Office gave permission for council workers to come in for the repairs. There was a plague of mice too.

He'd had prosthetic arms fitted, but
apparently when he was first arrested
the police smashed them. Brothers at the
mosque collected money and he had new
ones fitted. But the police smashed those
too the second time he was arrested, he told
me.

CCTV film, black and white.

WOMAN B: Maybe we're both monsters now.
They have destroyed us as a family, your
Home Office with its Control Orders.
Inside this house when he was shut up with
us, he made another prison – for all of us.
He was violent. He wanted to control me,
my every move, and the children – what
they wore, who they saw, where we went.
Let him go away to his home – without us.

I want my life back.

WENDY: When he asked me to marry him, I
accepted without a moment's hesitation.
He's special, different from other men,
somehow. For one thing he's really good
at languages – unlike me. I have bought
an Arabic grammer, but somehow there's
always something I need to do rather than
that. I'll learn in talking though in the end.
I've told Mustapha he'll have to teach me.

Of course my children were shocked at my marriage, but they were not going to be too enamoured of me marrying someone who was supposed to be a terrorist – which of course he isn't – and also 5 years younger – I'm 67. But children come round.

My 91 year old mother has been wonderful about it, sent Mustafa a card, and some money. He asked for permission to meet her, but he wasn't given permission by the Home Office. And I wasn't given permission by the Home Office for us to be married properly – although I sent them the hundred and something pounds fee, and I never got it back. So we had an Islamic marriage.

ALEXIA: My mother and one of my sisters is cleared when they come to visit from France, and they can sleep here in the flat with me. But I have to tell the Home Office which day they would come and how long they would stay.

And my friend, she's clear now, it took them more than nine months to clear her. The thing is as well, some people, some of my friends here, don't like to be, to be cleared, and give the Home Office their ID. They don't like that, because they are scared that they will have trouble or something. When they see that my husband, without any evidence, he's in prison, he can be detained…… so they are scared for themselves as well. Because even without evidence, you go to prison. So people don't want that.

I speak to my mother every day, she's happy now that my husband is back here with me. She knows every small thing in my life.

WENDY: Then he was gone, deported – he just gave up his appeal to remain, couldn't stand it any more – the Control Order, the isolation, the waiting for court.

So, he's at home in Tiaret, and I think most of his friends have moved away. He does go out, often when I phone I can tell he's out, but he just says he's "turning around, turning around" – men…. they never tell you where they're going, what they're doing.

I can get a three month visa, and I go and visit for a month whenever I can. But I cant move to Algeria, I have to look after my mother.

I'm torn in two, looking after my mother, looking after Mustapha. He has Post Traumatic Stress Disorder, he gets really low periods, but he wont talk to me about anything in his past – I'd love to know about his past. But, you just have to take things as they are, don't you?

I really like Mustafa's family, I stay with them, there, in Tiaret, they're very, very kind. They are my family now. I'd like to go there for good.

It's hard here now. I cant wear a scarf, I just couldn't here where I live – its not London you know.

And even without that, people are not too nice. People know who I am. The other day a woman came right up to me in the street and said, "I think you're a fool, marrying like that, a real fool." Can you imagine?

Lots of people don't want to speak to me. Even muslims here don't want to know me. I'm quite isolated here.

Exit WENDY.

* * * * * *

All dark.

Black and white CCTV: A completely veiled woman in black, sitting, camera blurred, close up .

WOMAN A: I grew to hate him as he sat in prison year after year and I'm alone dealing with out of control children, failing exams, bed wetting, things I cant even say – my children mix with bad children in your schools here. I've got a family that's broken, children who know that I don't respect their father. What is my life now? I haven't even got a passport, a nationality. Are my solicitors really trying for me? For him?..... No, that's probably unfair, but that's how I am now, always angry. I'm not myself.

I cant remember happiness. I cant remember I loved it here in England and I felt safe for the first time in years. Noone is in limbo here like me now.

My heart is broken, no more good dreams for me..

YASMINE: This experience can make a person become another person…in fact I think they are trying to make us become another person.

Look at my house, how it is – I want it
tidy, with no pain, just to sit in peacefully
with my family – this country I came to
for refuge, for peace, is like my big house,
why would we want to spoil it any way? Be
terrorist? Look at this house, filled with all
these little children of my daughters, this is
my world – new babies, school, dinosaurs,
little cars. Why is my husband missing
all this life? And my daughters, so much
tension for them, their lives are being eaten
by this. Imagine their little boys asking, why
is Grandpa not here, can we give pocket
money to a man to give him back?

SABAH: One time my solicitor brought me a
report about Guantanamo from the Tipton
people. It was so bad what they said about
my husband's health, and about what
happen inside there. What Americans do
to men. …I cant bear it, but I cant show
anything in front of the children. I go to
sit in the park where the children run and
don't see my face. I cant tell my mother, I
don't want her to worry, though sometimes
she hears from my voice.

I have to be so careful for everyone, the
children, my Mum, my husband, his family.
Never say a negative word, never show
what I feel.

I tell him in my letters, don't worry, the children are good, they do well in school, the littlest ones are funny, I'm fine. Your wife is still patient, you'll be strong too. I want to push him, be strong, Allah will help you with this test.

Inside I'm crying. I tell myself, don't be sad, its stupid, you have only one life, don't throw it away in sadness.

I can only pray. I know Allah is doing this test for me, for him, for a reason.

I read Koran, and read, and pray for strength.

One time the lawyers arranged permission so I could speak to my husband on the telephone after all these years...... There no words for the emotion when I heard his voice.........

CCTV of SABAH walking in Grosvenor Square, then inside the US embassy, then on the phone, first very calm, then puts phone down, crying and crying

Afterwards I went home to the children and I told them, Dad is fine, don't worry, he'll come soon, he kisses you all, he knows you are good children. You'll see him soon.

Then in the mosque for Eid, people kept coming to me and hugging me, saying how good for the telephone call with your husband. They were kind and happy for me....

But noone knows except Allah what is happening for me, what is in my heart.

CCTV WOMAN Z, loose Indian scarf

Once, a long time ago, my husband wrote this letter to me from Guantanamo:

"I am dying here every day, mentally and physically. This is happening to all of us. We have been ignored, locked up in the middle of the ocean for years. Rather than humiliate myself, having to beg for water, I would rather hurry up the process that is going to happen anyway. I would like to die quietly, by myself. I was once 250 pounds. I dropped to 150 pounds in the first hunger strike. I want to make it easy on everyone. I want no feeding, no forced tubes, no "help", no "intensive assisted feeding". This is my legal right. The British government refuses to help me. What is the point of my wife being British? I thought Britain stood for justice, but they abandoned us, people who have lived in Britain for years, and who have British wives and children. I hold the British government responsible for my death, as I do the Americans."

My own husband wrote this………….

Why do they not help him? Why have the others come back and not him? Can you tell me? Why can no one tell me? … I cant believe my own husband wrote that letter about wanting to die – he's not like that. He's big, and strong, and talking, always talking to everyone, making friends with everyone – people always love him. You couldn't not love him.

I prayed when I went on the Hadj to let me marry a man in white robes and a scarf like those I saw – my prayer was answered back home in Battersea – a young man from Medina came to the mosque and someone spoke to my mother. I liked him when I saw him, though I did think at first he was just too big…but he was too kind to me not to love him.

You know, now I have dreams, I hear voices, bad voices in my head, they tell me he is dead, or that he has divorced me. I try to tell them to go away, but they come back again. They aren't true are they?

What is happening to me?

You know, now he's been away from me in Guantanamo longer than we were together – eight years. And my youngest boy, he never saw his Dad, he doesn't even know what a Dad is.

SABAH: All these years and tests show things you'd not know before.

I see things with different eyes. If I see a
carrot – I only see orange, orange, and what
it means for me…for my husband.

Now I'm very tired and very sensitive.
Allah knows how much I am exhausted.
Noone else can know these suffering years.

I love my husband so much, and I know
he loves me, and our children, so much.
Nothing has changed for us. When I see his
letter, his writing, well, how to tell you how
happy I am……..

But, you know, he's changed too, he's
written me poems, and for the children,
something he never did before. When
I read a letter from him, I can be so, so
happy, he advises me, he has advice for
each child, I can tell he is still strong after
all these years and everything they did to
him.

I pray to Allah, please help me, and help all
those who are suffering and noone knows
their story.

NOUR: Two years ago, after I went home for
the summer, I left my eldest daughter at
home, there in Jordan with my mother – for
me to leave her……, for me to be without
her……only a mother could know what it
means, but it's a better life for her there I
thought, a normal life for a child, even if
it meant being without her mother. It was
such a hard, hard decision.

Then last year I left the second one, she's a very brilliant child, she does so well at school, but here all the restrictions of her life, because of her father, like no Internet, stress every minute, she doesn't do as well as she could, like other children, and the tension, the tension, in the house,....... of course I could see it was holding her back.

The older one, I think she's more emotionally affected by everything that's happened, she needs her mother.......

I'm torn, should I bring her back into all this conflict and difficult life? Should I? My head gives me a different answer every five minutes. Its all my responsibility..... all of them, even my husband, are my responsibility.

SABAH: After 5 years without ever seeing Dad, just hearing about him all the time, my little girl asked me, why do my friends come to nursery with Mum and Dad? Why am I only with Mum?

And she gets confused about Dad and God. She asks Dad to make a nice sunny day when its holidays, and the other children laugh at him and say, Dad cant do that, that's God.

The third one, he's seven now, and he tells me, I want to do karate, I want to be strong, to make a team to go and bring my dad home. I tell him, 'No, no, force is not the way.'

Then, he worries, 'when I grow up to be a man, will I be in prison too? Did my Dad do something bad?

It's all too early for them.......

I try, I advise myself to try, not to watch TV any more, except cartoons for the children, its too much, everywhere blood and pain for Muslims – Iraq, Palestine, Afghanistan. I tell myself, think of flowers, of trees, of beautiful things, try to relax. But, then.......

My children, even the little one, they see those orange suits on TV, and they say, is it Daddy, I tell them no, no, he's not like that, your Dad.

For years I didn't tell them anything about Guantanamo, just that Dad had a problem with his passport and would come soon.

But now they know. They know too many things.

The oldest, in the last two years he's done so many media, and reading in meetings letters he wrote to his Dad. He wants to do it – for his Dad as he's the oldest, but also it makes him angry when nothing happens.

He's a child.......but he hasn't had a childhood for half of his little life.

NOUR: My children, like all children, they want their parents together. But they have to know what is happening, they must know, so they can cope with this life.......

I don't have brothers here, I don't have sisters, if anything happened to me, what then for my children?

I talk to my father and my brothers on the phone, I ask them why they chose my husband. They didn't even know him well then – and they certainly don't know him now, after what Britain has done to him, filling him with anger, rotting his life.

In Islam you're supposed to just accept, however hard your life is with your husband – no man is perfect. Sometimes, I don't even like speaking to my family on the phone. They just don't know what its like living here in my situation, like this, how could they understand, or even imagine it?

She puts on her veil, and leaves.

ALEXIA: My husband, before, he was very joyful, always laughing, just like my baby Ismael now – though Ismael is naughty. It was very nice when we were first together, very happy. When he came out of prison he became paranoid. He was always thinking everybody is watching him even here at home, and the time he goes outside he is always scared.

He's doing nightmares, he's screaming
at night, he was too much seeing people
coming, he has medication and once
they sent him to a mental hospital, but he
couldn't stay there, he was locked up all the
time.

Now he don't speak much, like before. He's
closing himself off. Even from me.

It's difficult, it's difficult.

And any time he start to be better, there
is something that come, and he go back
to point zero. Our lives can't be balanced
because anything that will happen in this
country – like when 7/7 happened – he can
go back to prison. For what?

SABAH: My boys, now they don't want anyone
coming to the house and speaking about
their Dad –they want the whole story to
go away. They wont let any boys at school
mention their Dad.

In the early years, when they didn't know
about Guantanamo, and I didn't have any
letters from my husband for three years,
they used to call out from the garden when
they saw a plane, is Dad in that one? And
when we moved house they became very,
very anxious – how will Dad find us? How
will he know the new address? I would tell
them, don't worry, he'll find us.

ALEXIA: He lost all his trust in this country. Now they even want to send him back to a country that everyone knows has a bad record on human rights. Those who went back to Algeria from here, some are in prison and we hear about their torture, and the informers who tell false stories because they too were tortured. It's too much, he doesn't trust any more.

If he goes to any country now, they will know the label 'terrorist' that the British put on him, it's following him everywhere.

We know we can't stay here……we would like to go to any country that would accept us. To live freely without any control, that's what we need. We'd be happy to accept any country. But which would accept us? That's the question.

I'd like very much to be in my country, Senegal, but not just Senegal, any country that would have us, where we can have a normal life. Any country. Because I think this is very priceless.

Anywhere you can live free, we are happy to go.

Exit ALEXIA.

YASMINE: Before, I had hope, now I've lost it. We live like over a volcano. Where is our place in this world? We have made life here. I am British, all my children, my thirteen grandchildren – British. Why is my husband not allowed to be with us here? How can it be that he's supposed to go to Jordan, in his wheelchair, with all his health dramas to cope with? Alone? Or am I to uproot the five families of my daughters, with their husbands from Germany, Algeria, Morocco, Egypt – all made lives here?

SABAH: After years my husband was officially cleared in Guantanamo by the Americans, he's not an enemy combatant…….. after all these years. So, they *really* know he's innocent – but of course they knew that all the time.

When the children heard he'd been cleared, they started asking, when , when will he come? Can we have a party immediately for him – when's he coming? Who will bring him? Will he come by train or car? They thought it would be now, today, tomorrow. And they wanted to go on television and thank everybody, every single person who helped us.

After I heard he was cleared I never leave
my mobile out of my hand, every minute,
just like at the very beginning. When will I
hear something? Will the British bring him
back here now? I feel it is as though you try
to visit someone, and they keep saying, no,
no. In the end you don't even want to go to
their house. You ask and ask, and they keep
saying they don't want you.

Is it normal to be begging to live with your
family? When he is completely innocent?
Will something more, bad, happen to him?
We don't know anything.....still, after all
these years, noone tells us.

What's this democracy, what's this justice,
they talk so much about?

Because my husband's more than two years
away he doesn't have the right to come
back as a resident. And why was he away
for two years? Was it a picnic? A night club?
They know why he was away.

The justice in your courts of justice, it
doesn't exist.

*CCTV Amani – not veiled, very chic, looks straight
into the camera*

We kept writing to the Foreign Office and they sent back these standard letters saying, 'You should seek help from your brother's own country, his own government.' Which was so outrageous and so offensive. We told them that he's a refugee and that he's under threat from the Libyan government. It was a really, really depressing period, to be honest. It was so hopeless, and there's nowhere you can go, really, for help.

I left my work – the law – helping asylum seekers, because of the way I was feeling about this whole Guantanamo thing. Everyone in the family was expecting so much of me, and I felt like such a failure – I'm helping all these people who have a much less distressing sort of situation, and then I can't do anything for my own brother.

I felt really useless.

My way of dealing with it was to just forget about it as much as possible and do my own thing, have a baby, go out with my friends, don't talk about it.

I even used to have rows with my husband when he would print off things from the computer about Guantanamo to show me, like the Supreme Court decision in 2004 giving the detainees the right to appear in a US court, but I just felt it was all pointless.

Well, it *was* pointless – no prisoner ever got to appear, did they?.

The worst thing for me is not just the British failure all these years to take up Omar's case, its bigger then that. I can't believe the level of hypocrisy. I'm so disgusted with the façade they have of respect for human rights, and going to all these countries and teaching them to value human rights, while at the same time being complicit with what's happening to people in Guantanamo. The British are part of the torture indirectly.

SABAH: My little girl asks me now, why he doesn't come home now? She's angry, and she's thinking all the time, in the shower, every minute – why you don't know his address? Every night now, she's lying down next to me, she holds my face in her hands before she sleeps and says to me, why you don't know his address? When is he coming? When? When?

Waiting….noone knows what waiting is. Today I am waiting 2,800 days. Who can imagine even one hundred days of waiting?

I don't care for myself, just the children. Nothing makes me happy any more.

I still say, thanks God for every minute, thanks for everything, but I'm tired and sad.

Nobody can see my heart.

This time will stay in my heart for ever. Even when my children grow up and have their happy lives, it'll be in my memory.

I need a small corner of the world with my children and my husband – to sit and be relaxed, and live a simple life.

I try to forget. I must forget. I must forgive.

She reaches for her white veil, and sits there as she puts it on.

Dark.

Background image of SABAH, in long black coat and white veil, taken from the back, with her five children, walking across a London park.

FEMALE VOICEOVER: Sabah's husband, and Amani's brother, were returned to Britain from Guantanamo Bay in late 2007.

Yasmine's husband had his deportation order dropped in early 2009.

Alexia is still in limbo, fighting against her husband's deportation to Algeria, and has had another baby.

Nour took her children back to live in Jordan in 2009.

Wendy is still periodically visiting her husband in Algeria.

Woman Z's husband is still in Guantanamo Bay